THE MAIN EVENT

THE MOVES AND MUSCLE OF PRO WRESTLING

Patrick Jones

M MILLBROOK PRESS · MINNEAPOLIS

Millbrook Press
A division of Lerner Publishing Group, Inc.
241 First Avenue North
Minneapolis, MN 55401 U.S.A.

Website address: www.lernerbooks.com

Library of Congress Cataloging-in-Publication Data

Jones, Patrick.
   The main event : the moves and muscle of pro wrestling / by Patrick Jones.
      p.   cm.   —   (Spectacular sports)
   Includes index.
   ISBN 978–0–7613–8635–3 (lib. bdg. : alk. paper)
   1. Wrestling—History. I. Title.
GV1195.J67 2013
796.812—dc23   2011046180

Manufactured in the United States of America
1 – DP – 7/15/12

CONTENTS

WWE superstar Shawn Michaels battles the Undertaker *(standing)* during the 2010 WrestleMania event. In this move, the wrestler lifts his opponent on his shoulders and drops him face-first onto the turnbuckle.

INTRODUCTION:

IT'S TIME FOR THE MAIN EVENT

In 1911 more than 30,000 fans jammed Comiskey Park in Chicago, Illinois, to watch a wrestling card. The night's main event featured Frank Gotch and George Hackenschmidt. The audience cheered wildly as Gotch and Hackenschmidt walked to the ring. There was no music or fireworks. They wore no elaborate costumes. Each man dressed simply in black wrestling trunks and black wrestling shoes.

Almost one hundred years later, 72,000 fans filled the University of Phoenix Stadium in Arizona for WWE's (formerly World Wrestling Entertainment) annual WrestleMania event. After 10 matches, it was time for the main event. Shawn Michaels entered to his theme music while a video played on the big screen called the TitanTron. He posed in the ring as fireworks exploded. A loud chime rang to announce his opponent, the Undertaker. Inside the ring, the Undertaker stared at the camera that broadcast the match to millions of fans across the globe. It was the match fans had been waiting for. The Undertaker had never lost at WrestleMania, but Michaels vowed to end the streak. Michaels was so confident that he put his career on the line, promising to leave WWE if he lost the match. The hard-hitting action lasted for 20 minutes before the Undertaker finished off Michaels to win the biggest match of 2010.

For more than 100 years, pro wrestling has entertained countless millions of fans. They are drawn to wrestling's characters, action, and dramatic stories. Many people argue that wrestling is staged, and not a real sport. But to true wrestling fans, that doesn't matter. Even the WWE admits it—the company refers to its product as *sports entertainment*, not as a sport. Fans understand. They know what wrestling is all about: Two men, one ring. The main event.

Wrestling has existed for centuries. This British watercolor sketch from the early 1800s shows two men at a wrestling match.

THE HISTORY OF WRESTLING:

FROM ANCIENT GREECE TO PAY-PER-VIEW

Many believe that wrestling is the world's oldest sport. It is simple. It takes only two people and requires no equipment. Early wrestling didn't even have any rules! Almost every ancient culture created artwork showing wrestlers. Wrestling was especially popular in ancient Greece and Rome. Greek mythology is filled with wrestling stories. It was said that Theseus, the king of Athens, Greece, first introduced rules in wrestling.

The first professional wrestlers performed at carnivals in Europe. They used a style called catch wrestling. The name is believed to have come from the phrase, "catch as catch can," which was a way of saying that a wrestler was allowed to hold any part of his opponent's body. Europeans brought the sport to the United States, where it quickly caught on. Abraham Lincoln was a catch wrestler before he was president of the United States! The popular style in the United States soon changed to collar-and-elbow wrestling. Matches began with wrestlers holding each other's collars and elbows.

Carnival wrestling grew popular in the United States after the Civil War (1861–1865). The carnival wrestler issued a challenge to wrestle a fan. If the fan won, he got a prize. Other fans bet on the outcome. Carnival wrestlers usually let the fan win, but the carnival made money from bets.

WRESTLING BOOM

By 1900, interest in sports—including wrestling—in the Unites States was on the rise. The first match between U.S. champion Frank Gotch and European champ George Hackenschmidt in 1908 drew 30,000 people, as did the 1911 rematch. (Gotch won both matches.) When Gotch retired in 1913, wrestling went into a slump. Ed "Strangler" Lewis came onto the scene in the 1920s to revive the sport. Lewis dominated, both in the ring and behind the scenes. Lewis, his manager Billy Sandow, and promoter Joseph "Toots" Mondt became known as the Gold Dust Trio for their ability to make money in wrestling.

The Gold Dust Trio created the modern pro wrestling show. Masked and costumed wrestlers didn't just exchange holds on the mat. Instead, they punched, kicked, and slammed each other. Flying dropkicks and other exciting moves thrilled the crowd. Personalities were as important as victories. Outcomes were predetermined. The goal was not to win but to entertain the crowd.

Ed "Strangler" Lewis *(left)* puts his opponent in a headlock. This match took place in Michigan City, Indiana, in 1925.

During the Great Depression (1929–1942), many people were out of work and struggled to feed their families. While many sports suffered during this time, wrestling fared well. People who felt powerless in their lives could cheer when the good guy (baby face) defeated the bad guy (heel). In addition, wrestling promoters found new ways to make matches more interesting. They invented tag team wrestling, which put four wrestlers in the ring—sometimes all at the same time! Shows featured a great variety of competitors. Such wrestlers as little people, women, and sometimes even bears thrilled crowds. Wrestlers gave elaborate interviews to win fans or elicit boos. In a few years, the sport had changed from two men wrestling on a mat for hours to a quick-hitting show filled with action and characters.

WRESTLING COMES TO TV

This combination of action and characters made professional wrestling a perfect fit for early network television in the late 1940s. Additionally, it was cheap and easy to produce (make and pay for)—a big bonus for networks. Fans who had never paid to see a show could watch for free on TV. Lou Thesz, high-flying Antonio Rocca, and other

baby faces battled against Gorgeous George, Killer Kowalski, and other heels in worked matches (matches in which winners were predetermined by the wrestling company). But as TV matured, it no longer needed cheap, easy-to-produce programs. Wrestling became less popular. By the late 1950s, it was nowhere to be found on network TV.

Fans got thrills, chills, and spills watching professional wrestling matches ringside or on TV. In this 1953 match, Killer Kowalski (left) gets belted by his opponent, Verne Gagne, after Kowalski had been disqualified for bad behavior.

LADIES IN THE RING

When most people think of pro wrestling, they think of big, burly men. But women have enjoyed success in wrestling as well. The first women's champion recognized by most promoters was Mildred Burke. She held the World Women's Championship title from 1937 to 1954. But Burke was not allowed to wrestle in some states because they banned women's wrestling. The most famous woman wrestler was Mary Lillian Ellison. She began her career as a valet (female manager) but soon wrestled as the Fabulous Moolah *(below, in the air)*. She won her first title in 1956, was still champion in 1985, and won her last match in 2003 at the age of 80! Valets were common in the 1980s, with WWE's Miss Elizabeth being the most famous. WWE began calling women wrestlers "divas" in the 1990s. Divas appear on both *Raw* and *Smackdown*. Diva matches have also become a staple of PPV events.

For the next 30 years, small wrestling companies grew popular in different regions of the country. Many cities had their own promotions, TV shows, and stars. These promotions were often part of a larger organization. The country was divided between three large organizations: the American Wrestling Association (AWA) in the Midwest, the World Wide Wrestling Federation (WWWF, present-day WWE) in the East, and the National Wrestling Alliance (NWA) in the rest of the country. Wrestlers performed in one promotion and then moved onto the next. The NWA was the biggest, with its champion defending his title all over the world. But WWE made the most money. And it was about to make even more.

THE RISE OF WWE

The first cable wrestling show debuted (first appeared) on the TBS station out of Georgia in 1976. In the early 1980s, the WWE, under the leadership of Vince McMahon, became the first successful national promotion. By 1984 WWE had two cable shows as well as shows on local stations across the country. McMahon was determined to run the competition into the ground. He became famous for poaching (hiring) wrestlers from other promotions, including Hulk Hogan from AWA and Roddy Piper from NWA.

McMahon was always thinking big. In 1985 he hatched the idea of a wrestling event broadcast nationwide on closed-circuit TV. This type of broadcast could be shown in theaters or on the big screens of arenas nationwide. Then WWE could sell lots more tickets—and make a lot more money. McMahon promoted the event on the Music Television (MTV) network. In February 1985, MTV broadcast a match between Hogan and Piper, dubbed the Brawl to Settle It All. The match drew a record rating on MTV, but it was really just a setup for the main event: WrestleMania.

About 19,000 fans flocked to New York City's Madison Square Garden in March 1985 to witness the first WrestleMania. A million more watched on closed-circuit broadcast at theaters and arenas across the United States and Canada. McMahon knew that he had to give fans a spectacle, so he brought in celebrities—most notably actor Mr. T. The idea of mixing celebrities with wrestling has continued in every WrestleMania since.

McMahon kept finding new ways to bring in money. Two years later, 1987's WrestleMania drew more than 90,000 to the live show. But McMahon also offered the show to fans at home via a new technology called pay-per-view (PPV). PPV allowed fans to pay to have the show broadcast to their own TV sets. Once again, McMahon had opened up a whole new market, and wrestling would never be the same.

Mr. T and "Rowdy" Roddy Piper face off during a WrestleMania match in Madison Square Garden in 1985.

THE RATINGS WARS

McMahon continued to expand, securing a spot on network TV with NBC's *Saturday Night's Main Event*. Wrestling even returned to prime-time TV in 1988. About 33 million viewers watched WWE champ Hulk Hogan lose his title to Andre the Giant.

McMahon and WWE were dominating the pro wrestling scene, driving out many competitors. But some other promotions still survived. In the South, Jim Crockett Jr. enjoyed success with Mid-Atlantic Championship Wrestling, which was broadcast on Ted Turner's TBS network. The promotion was able to compete due in part to the popularity of its stars, including Ric Flair and Sting. In 1988 Crockett sold the promotion to Turner, who renamed it World Championship Wrestling (WCW).

As WCW rose in popularity, WWE struggled. Hogan and other headliners left WWE for WCW. New WCW president Eric Bischoff took on WWE directly in fall 1995 by putting his new TV show, *WCW Monday Nitro*, on at the same time as WWE's *Monday Night Raw*. The Monday-night wars were on! In summer 1996, former WWE wrestlers Kevin Nash and Scott Hall showed up on *Nitro*, bragging that they would take over WCW. At the next WCW PPV event, longtime baby face Hulk Hogan turned on his fans and became a heel. With Hall and Nash, Hogan formed the New World Order (NWO) faction (group of wrestlers). The NWO angle was a huge success, and WCW thrived.

WCW was giving WWE a taste of its own medicine, poaching many of WWE's biggest stars. McMahon was having money troubles, and soon he couldn't pay his most popular wrestler, WWE champ Bret Hart. Hart decided to leave the company but refused to lose his WWE title. McMahon had to do something, so he planned a whole new angle for WWE in hopes of igniting fan interest. In November 1997, Hart wrestled Shawn Michaels in Montreal, Canada. Hart went into the match believing that he was supposed to win. But McMahon changed the plan without letting Hart in on the secret, costing him the title belt.

In just a few years, Vince McMahon turned his father's small company into the world's biggest wrestling promotion.

Becoming actively involved in his program was a risky move for McMahon. For years he had appeared on TV as an announcer. But as a result of the Hart incident, McMahon revealed himself as the WWE owner (which hadn't been widely known). Most fans hated what McMahon did to Hart, so McMahon channeled that hatred. He took on the persona of the evil Mr. McMahon and became WWE's number one heel. In wrestling every heel needs a baby face to battle. Enter Stone Cold Steve Austin! The feud between McMahon and Austin would turn the fortune of WWE and make Austin the most popular wrestler in the world.

Wrestling fans *loved* Austin. They cheered him on as he won his first WWE title, defeating Shawn Michaels at 1998's WrestleMania. (The match famously included boxer Mike Tyson as a guest referee.) After WrestleMania, McMahon tried to turn the "redneck" Austin into a "corporate champion" who would follow McMahon's orders. But the trash-talking Austin was not one to obey authority—much to the delight of his fans. The feud between Austin and Mr. McMahon lasted for years and led to WWE overtaking WCW in TV ratings. Once again, WWE boasted a stable of stars, including Austin, the Rock, Mankind, and the Undertaker. The content of WWE TV shows became more adult in what McMahon dubbed the Attitude Era. McMahon cashed in on the growing popularity by selling shares of the company's stock to the public. Soon he was a billionaire!

WWE NATION

By 2000 interest in wrestling was at an all-time high. The Rock hosted *Saturday Night Live* before 2000's WrestleMania. Austin and the Rock both starred in movies, while WCW produced a wrestling movie called *Ready to Rumble*. WCW also put celebrities such as basketball player Dennis Rodman and late-night talk show host Jay Leno in the ring. Actor David Arquette even won the WCW title!

Even though WCW's wrestlers included old favorites Hulk Hogan and Ric Flair, as well as up-and-comers such as Bill Goldberg, WCW could no longer compete with WWE. In March 2001, McMahon bought WCW and closed down the promotion. Many WCW wrestlers joined WWE right away as part of the Invasion angle. The feud between WWE wrestlers and WCW wrestlers led to a ratings spike.

But not all was well. Critics said that WWE's Attitude Era shows were too violent and mature for kids. They argued that wrestling promoted violence and bullying. Controversy continued as many WWE wrestlers and former wrestlers died young. WWE officials quickly responded to the problem by taming down the content to make it more kid-friendly. Perhaps because of the content change, the popularity of wrestling declined after 2001. By 2004 WWE had lost two of its biggest stars. Austin retired due to injuries, and the Rock moved on to a film career. However, a few new stars were on their way to take their place.

The Rock is pictured on stage during a March 2000 episode of *Saturday Night Live*. He went on to have a successful acting career after his retirement from professional wrestling.

John Cena became one of professional wrestling's superstars in the twenty-first century.

The Rock retired after 2004's WrestleMania. On the same card were two wrestlers making their WrestleMania debut: John Cena and Randy Orton. These two young superstars would become the new faces of WWE. Cena and Orton would battle other up-and-comers such as Batista and Rey Mysterio, as well as established stars like the Undertaker and Triple H.

Meanwhile, McMahon continued to innovate. With WCW out of business, he created his own competition by dividing his company into two brands: Raw and Smackdown. Except during PPV events, wrestlers appeared either on the *Monday Night Raw* or *Smackdown*. Each year, shortly after WrestleMania, the brands held a draft to move wrestlers from one show to the other. WWE also produced new TV shows, including *Tough Enough*, a contest to recruit new talent to WWE. The show introduced fans to several future WWE stars, including the Miz.

McMahon has always been a pioneer in wrestling, and that continues into the present day. WWE rakes in millions from merchandise, including T-shirts, books, and DVDs. Most wrestlers have their own Web pages, Twitter accounts, and Facebook pages. WWE and its stars take every opportunity to connect fans across the globe.

2 TEN GREAT MAIN EVENTS

Wrestling main events aren't like championships in other sports. They're more like a movie in which two characters have a conflict. The twists and turns in the story leading up to the conflict are as interesting and important as the final fight. What matters in these 10 great main events isn't each hold or slam but how the match—and the story surrounding it—advanced pro wrestling. These 10 matches helped make professional wrestling what it is today.

FRANK GOTCH VS. GEORGE HACKENSCHMIDT
CHICAGO, 1908 AND 1911

The 1908 match between the European champ Hackenschmidt and U.S. champ Gotch was pro wrestling's first great dream match. It pitted the Iowa farm boy Gotch against "the Russian Adonis" Hackenschmidt. Gotch was short and powerful, while Hackenschmidt was tall and sculpted. In this first big main event, these two very different men wrestled for the title before a packed stadium. That basic formula has not changed much over the years!

George Hackenschmidt and Frank Gotch took to the ring in Chicago in September 1911. The second time the duo met, many felt that the outcome had been fixed.

More than 30,000 fans filled Dexter Park Pavilion in Chicago to watch the match. Hackenschmidt was favored due to his powerful bear hug hold. But Gotch escaped Hackenschmidt's holds, slipping out of his grasp time and time again. After two hours, Hackenschmidt grew tired. This allowed Gotch to win the first fall. At this time, wrestling matches were two out of three falls. A wrestler had to beat his foe twice to get the win. The two wrestlers went to the dressing room between falls. The crowd was stunned when Hackenschmidt would not come out for the second fall. He claimed Gotch cheated by oiling his body to slip out of holds and using illegal moves. Hackenschmidt refused to wrestle against a cheater.

Gotch avoided a rematch for three years, but the wrestling fans demanded the two meet again. Finally, in 1911, the rematch was on. They battled again in front of another Chicago crowd of more than 30,000. Or did they? Weeks before the match, Hackenschmidt hurt his knee in training. He wanted to back out, but promoters told him they would fix the match so he would win one fall. But nobody told Gotch about that plan! Gotch took down the injured Hackenschmidt, who couldn't defend himself. Fans had come expecting to see a classic match. Instead, they left angry over the one-sided nature of the bout. Reporters heard rumors about the match being fixed, and soon many newspapers stopped covering wrestling as a sport.

STRANGLER LEWIS VS. JIM LONDOS
CHICAGO, 1934

For most of the 1920s, big, strong Ed "Strangler" Lewis ruled wrestling. There was nothing fancy about Lewis. He was all about power moves, including a side headlock to choke out his foes. But in the early 1930s, newcomer Jim Londos was the fresh face of wrestling. When the two met, it was a classic theme in wrestling: the tough veteran defending his title against the young, often handsome, newcomer.

Pro wrestling had changed since the days of Gotch and Hackenschmidt. Wrestling promoters controlled the sport. Promoters determined when and where matches would take place and even who would win them. Lewis represented the Gold Dust Trio, while Londos represented a group of New York promoters. Both Lewis and Londos claimed to be the real world champion. Only a main event could settle the debate.

Strangler Lewis puts Jim Londos in a headlock.

The match was held at Chicago's Wrigley Field in September 1934. At first, newspapers largely ignored the bout. By this time, the media and most knowledgeable fans had figured out that wrestling matches were fixed. But promoter Toots Mondt told reporters that Lewis and Londos would wrestle for real, without a fixed outcome, and the better man would win. With that hype, the interest in the match exploded. More than

35,000 fans attended, paying a combined $96,000! It would not be until 1952 that a wrestling match would make more money.

But Mondt had lied to reporters. Lewis and Londos were professional wrestlers whose job it was to put on a show, not engage in a real fight. Lewis was in control during most of the match, but Londos escaped his headlocks. After fighting outside the ring, Londos body-slammed Lewis to the mat and applied a hammerlock by grabbing Lewis's arm and twisting it behind his back. With Lewis in pain, Londos forced the Strangler's shoulders to the mat for the three count. In just under 50 minutes, the young cub had defeated the old lion. That same story line would repeat again and again over the decades.

LOU THESZ VS. EDOUARD CARPENTIER CHICAGO, 1957

From 1949 through 1956, Lou Thesz was the undisputed NWA world champion. He went from city to city challenging anyone who claimed to be the world champion. These main events to unify (combine) two titles resulted in two things: sold-out arenas and Thesz having his hand raised in victory. His 1952 match in Los Angeles against Baron Leone was the first match to draw $100,000. Still, some promoters thought Thesz was dull. They wanted a flashier champ.

Edouard Carpentier, nicknamed the Flying Frenchman, fit that bill. Carpentier took to the air with dropkicks, cartwheels, and flying headscissors. Like Rey Mysterio years later, Carpentier changed the idea of what wrestling could be. Fans flocked to sold-out arenas to see his acrobatic style. Many promoters wanted him to be the champ, rather than the mat wrestler Thesz.

The clash between the contrasting styles of these two men would become another staple main event. Fans liked both wrestlers. That meant it was a rare baby face matchup in which each wrestler was considered a good guy. The champ Thesz tied up Carpentier with mat holds. When the challenger escaped, he would counter with a flying move.

Lou Thesz unleashed an array of dramatic moves on his opponent Edouard Carpentier. In the end, however, Carpentier took home the championship belt *(left)* in a disputed match.

As with most main events at the time, the first wrestler to win two falls would be the victor. After 20 minutes, Thesz won the first fall by using a flying body press—a move many would have expected out of Carpentier! After a brief rest period, the grapplers hooked up again. Carpentier exploded with a series of flying moves, winning the second fall in less than four minutes. As the bell rang to begin the third fall, Thesz remained in his corner. One of Carpentier's acrobatic moves had hurt his back. The referee ended the match because of the champ's injury.

Wrestling titles at that time could only change hands if the champ were pinned or submitted. No rule addressed a champ who had to bow out of a match due to injury. Many promoters thought Carpentier was the true champ, while others sided with Thesz. It was not the first time that two wrestlers both claimed to be champion, and it would not be the last.

RIC FLAIR VS. HARLEY RACE, GREENSBORO, 1983

Even though WWE was gaining in popularity in the 1980s, most fans still viewed the NWA Championship as the most important title. From the late 1970s to the early 1980s, Harley Race dominated the NWA. He won the NWA title six times. Race was known for being one of the toughest men in wrestling. One of his most

Even when he was on the receiving end of a piledriver, Ric Flair *(in red)* was hard to defeat.

famous moves was diving from the top rope onto his opponent, using his head as a weapon!

Ric Flair was everything that Race wasn't. With his bleached blond hair, expensive clothes, and skills on the microphone, Flair was an entertainer. He'd held the NWA title once before, but Race took it from him in June 1983. Flair demanded a rematch, while Race offered $50,000 to any wrestler who injured Flair. Many tried, including Bob Orton Jr. (father to present-day star Randy Orton), but none could finish off Flair.

With interest in the match growing, promoter Jim Crockett knew that it was too big for one arena. When he set the match between Flair and Race in North Carolina, he broadcast it via closed circuit to arenas in other states. The men wrestled inside a cage on Thanksgiving night in 1983. Former NWA champ Gene Kiniski was the special ref for the cage match, but he could maintain little control as Race and Flair battled. Before long, both were bleeding as they rammed each other's faces into the cage.

After 30 minutes, Flair climbed to the top rope to dive on Race. But Race was ready and caught Flair. Before Race could slam Flair, he tripped over Kiniski, who had been knocked down. Flair fell on top of Race, and Kiniski counted to three. Flair was the champ for the second time! It was the match that showed the world that a great main event could be too big for just one small arena.

HULK HOGAN VS. ANDRE THE GIANT
DETROIT, 1987

Andre the Giant was the biggest WWE star of the 1970s. He earned that honor not only because he never lost a big main event match but also because of his size. At 7 feet 4 inches (2.2 meters) and more than 500 pounds (227 kilograms), Andre was the world's largest athlete. While Hulk Hogan was a big man—6 feet 8 inches (2 m), 300 pounds (136 kg), and with 24-inch (61-centimeter) biceps—he looked small compared to Andre. By the 1980s, Hogan had become wrestling's biggest star. As WWE champion, Hogan was a huge draw and was featured in the main event at the first two WrestleMania events.

The feud between Hogan and Andre started in January 1987 during Roddy Piper's interview show. Andre stunned Hogan and his fans by having the hated manager Bobby "the Brain" Heenan at his side. Andre challenged the champ to a title match. Then he attacked Hogan, ripping his shirt and leaving him bleeding. The stage was set.

On March 27, 1987, more than 93,000 fans packed the Silverdome in Pontiac, Michigan, to watch Hogan and Andre battle for the championship. The two exchanged

STARS AT WRESTLEMANIA

The first WrestleMania was the most important wrestling card ever. While wrestling cards had featured celebrities before, WrestleMania took it to a new level. Pop star Cyndi Lauper was a manager, baseball manager Billy Martin was ring announcer, and Las Vegas entertainer Liberace acted as timekeeper. Boxing great Muhammad Ali was the guest ref for the main event. In the main event, Hulk Hogan teamed with actor Mr. T., the star of the hit TV show *The A-Team*. The main event included a classic moment with Mr. T and Piper in the ring. Mr. T lifted Piper onto his shoulders and slammed him to the mat, to the delight of the fans. The tradition of including celebrities at WrestleMania has continued. In recent years, celebs such as billionaire Donald Trump and Snooki from the TV show *Jersey Shore* have made appearances.

punches. Then Hogan tried a body slam on Andre. But Hogan collapsed under Andre's weight and just escaped being pinned. Andre battered Hogan's back with stomps and punches. He locked Hogan into a bear hug submission hold, wrapping his huge arms around Hogan's waist and squeezed. The referee lifted Hogan's arm twice to make sure Hogan hadn't passed out. But before Hogan's arm dropped a third time, he punched his way out of the hold.

Just when Hogan looked defeated, he knocked Andre to the mat for the first time in the match. Andre slowly rose. Hogan scooped the Giant over

Andre the Giant has Hulk Hogan in a bear hug, nearly crushing Hogan, in the 1987 WrestleMania showdown.

his head and slammed the big man to the mat. Hogan bounced off the ropes and dropped his leg across Andre's throat and then covered him for the pin. Fans cheered as Hogan achieved the seemingly impossible by slamming and pinning the Giant, and the legend of Hulk Hogan grew.

SHAWN MICHAELS VS. BRET HART MONTREAL, 1997

If Andre and Hogan were the two biggest stars of their era, then Shawn Michaels and Bret Hart defined WWE in the 1990s. They both started as tag team wrestlers. When Hart won the WWE title, his first title defense on PPV was against Michaels. Michaels won his first WWE title at 1996's WrestleMania by defeating Hart in a match that lasted more than an hour!

By late 1996, a genuine rivalry between Hart and Michaels was growing. The two even had a real-life fight after an episode of *Monday Night Raw*. McMahon looked to capitalize on the interest in the rivalry by signing the two men to wrestle at 1997's Survivor Series in Montreal, Canada. Hart was a native Canadian, while Michaels often goaded Canadian fans by making fun of them. And if that drama wasn't enough, even more was happening behind the scenes. McMahon was in financial trouble and could no longer afford to pay Hart's salary. The fans didn't know it yet, but Hart would be leaving for WCW after the Survivor Series match. To make matters worse, Hart refused to lose his title to Michaels before he left the company.

Backstage, McMahon, Michaels, and others came up with a plan. McMahon promised Hart that he would not lose the title. The match would end in a disqualification. But McMahon, Michaels, and the match's referee didn't let Hart in on the real plan.

The wrestlers started with hard punches and kicks rather than holds. The action spilled out of the ring as Hart battered Michaels. Once back in the ring, Michaels put

Hart into Hart's own submission hold, the sharpshooter. With McMahon looking on at ringside, the ref ruled that Hart submitted and ended the match! Hart went crazy! He spat in McMahon's face and destroyed the area around the ring.

The Montreal match was the turning point in the WCW vs. WWE war. Many fans hated Vince McMahon because of his actions. And that was exactly what

Michaels and Hart battled many times in main events before their epic show in Montreal.

McMahon wanted. He took on the personality of the evil Mr. McMahon on TV and wrestling's number one heel. Soon, Stone Cold Steve Austin emerged as the baby face rival to McMahon. Their ongoing feud captured the attention of wrestling fans and changed the face of pro wrestling. But it all started in Montreal with Hart and Michaels.

GOLDBERG VS. HOLLYWOOD HULK HOGAN
ATLANTA, 1998

For more than a decade, fans had loved Hulk Hogan. But in summer 1996, Hogan turned his back on his fans and became the evil Hollywood Hulk Hogan. He formed the NWO faction, which dominated WCW.

While Hogan and the NWO won most of their matches, a new wrestler named Bill Goldberg won all his matches! Many of his matches lasted just minutes, and his foes rarely touched him. He was undefeated. Yet Hogan refused to defend his WCW title against Goldberg.

Fans kept the pressure on, and Hogan finally agreed to a match. It took place in June 1998 on *Monday Nitro*. More than 50,000 packed the Georgia Dome in Atlanta, Georgia. Hogan had lost very few matches in his career and rarely in the main event of a big show. For Goldberg, the match would be his first main event. Hogan bragged it would also be Goldberg's first loss.

Bill Goldberg acknowledges the crowd before his match with Hollywood Hulk Hogan in July 1998.

The fans at the Georgia Dome chanted, "Goldberg! Goldberg!" as the match drew on. Hogan relied on dirty tricks, such as gouging Goldberg's eyes. But Goldberg rallied behind the fan support. When Hogan missed his finishing move, the leg drop, Goldberg lifted him over his head and slammed him down for the three count. The delighted crowd let out a deafening roar of celebration.

The match between Goldberg and Hogan marked the high point for WCW. Afterward, it was downhill. The company finally went out of business in 2001. Goldberg and Hogan would join WWE later, but they never wrestled each other again. Their one and only match was a classic, as the young upstart hero did what few others had done: defeat the legendary Hulk Hogan.

STEVE AUSTIN VS. THE ROCK
SEATTLE, 2003

In the early 2000s, Rocky Maivia—better known as the Rock—was the WWE's rising star. He was a natural rival for Austin, and the two wrestled at the main events of the WrestleMania in 1999 and 2001. (Austin won both.) By 2003 both men were winding down their careers. Austin wanted one last great main event, while the Rock knew it was his last chance to beat Austin at WrestleMania.

The feud between Austin and the Rock raged for years, normally with Austin coming out on top.

In front of 60,000 fans at the Kingdome in Seattle, Washington, Austin and the Rock wrestled for the last time. Austin started fast, beating the Rock inside and outside of the ring. Just when it seemed Austin was in control, the Rock attacked Austin's legs. The Rock seemed ready to finish off Austin after slamming Austin's leg into the posts in the corner of the ring. But Austin fired back, using the Rock's own signature move, the rock bottom, to take control. The Rock countered by using Austin's stunner on him. Several times during the match, the ref counted as far as two on each wrestler. The Rock would not quit as he hit a third rock bottom and finally pinned Austin. While the match was not the final one of 2003's WrestleMania, for most fans it was the real main event.

JOHN CENA VS. TRIPLE H
CHICAGO, 2006

With the retirement of the Rock and Steve Austin, Triple H became WWE's biggest star. While Triple H battled in the main event at 2004's WrestleMania, newcomer John Cena was wrestling in the opening match. Even though Cena defeated Big Show to win the U.S. Championship, Cena wasn't happy. He wanted to be part of the main event.

During the first WWE draft in spring 2005, Cena moved to the Raw brand. There, he defended his title against Edge and Kurt Angle. But fans knew Cena wasn't really the champ until he beat Triple H. That set the stage for 2006's WrestleMania in Chicago.

Both wrestlers made grand entrances. Cena rode out in a vintage car like a 1930s mobster, while Triple H was carried to the ring on a throne. If the entrances were great, the match was even better. The action went back and forth with neither man gaining an advantage. Whenever Triple H tried a big move, Cena countered it. When Cena went for his finishing moves, Triple H escaped. After 20 minutes, Cena locked Triple H in his STF (stepover toehold facelock) submission hold, but Triple H escaped to the ropes. Back on their feet, Triple H went for his finishing move, the pedigree, only

John Cena *(left)* claimed the title belt from Triple H *(right)* after their first meeting in the ring in 2006.

to have Cena reverse it into another STF. Too far from the ropes, Triple H tapped out and gave Cena the first of many WrestleMania main event victories. With the win, Cena served notice that WWE had its next big star.

SHAWN MICHAELS VS. THE UNDERTAKER
PHOENIX, 2010

Before their 2010 main event at WrestleMania, Michaels and the Undertaker had a long history. Their first match in 1997 was so wild that both wrestlers were disqualified for fighting outside of the ring. For the rematch later in 1997, WWE needed a way to keep the action in the ring. And so the cell match was born! Cage matches had long been a WWE staple. But the steel cell had something a cage didn't—a top! Michaels and the Undertaker had another wild match, which Michaels won. A rematch at the 1998 Royal Rumble resulted in another Michaels victory.

Years passed before the two finally faced off again at WrestleMania in 2009. Each man claimed to be Mr. WrestleMania. Michaels claimed it because he had the most exciting matches at WrestleMania, but the Undertaker had an amazing 16–0 WrestleMania record. By the end of the night, he would be 17–0. He beat Michaels in one of the most dramatic WrestleMania matches ever, filled with big moves and near falls that had the 70,000-plus fans on the edges of their seats.

Michaels wanted a rematch. The Undertaker finally agreed but with one catch. Michaels had to put his career on the line. If he lost, he'd be forced to retire. The retirement match would be the main event for 2010's WrestleMania. Like the match the year before, each wrestler used every move he knew. At one point, with Michaels outside of the ring, the Undertaker hurled himself over the top rope and crashed onto Michaels! After 20 minutes of action, both wrestlers hit their finishing moves. Michaels landed his finisher, sweet chin music, but only got a two count. The Undertaker twice used his tombstone piledriver, but Michaels kicked out both times.

The Undertaker yelled for Michaels to "stay down," but Michaels would not quit. In a show of disrespect, Michaels slapped the Undertaker's face! The Undertaker grabbed Michaels for a third tombstone piledriver, finally pinning him for the win. Michaels was forced to retire, while the Undertaker's WrestleMania record improved to 18–0, leaving little doubt as to who the real Mr. WrestleMania was.

The Undertaker *(right)* flings Shawn Michaels over the ropes during their matchup in the 2010 WrestleMania.

3 THE STARS:
GREAT WRESTLERS OF THE PAST AND PRESENT

Professional wrestling is all about stars. Fans love to see hard punches, flying kicks, piledrivers, and other devastating moves, but it's the wrestlers that keep them coming back for more. It's more than just the moves that make a wrestler a star. A superstar needs the right look and the ability to captivate fans on the microphone. But above all, he needs the charisma to capture and hold fans' attention—whether they love him or hate him. From Frank Gotch to Randy Orton and so many of the champions in between, charisma makes stars, and stars make the main event.

FRANK GOTCH (1878–1917)

Born in a small Iowa town, Gotch wrestled his first match in 1899. He caught the attention of former champ Farmer Burns. After training with Burns, Gotch went to Alaska to take on all comers. When he returned, he challenged American champion Tom Jenkins. Gotch lost that match but won the rematch—and his first championship—in 1904. In 1908 he beat the formerly undefeated champion from Europe, George Hackenschmidt, in front of more than 30,000 people in Chicago. A rematch in 1911 saw another huge crowd and another Gotch victory. These victories turned Gotch from an athlete into a superstar. His fame made him, in a sense, the first modern pro wrestler. Gotch retired as champion in 1913.

STRANGLER LEWIS (1891–1966)

Ed Lewis had his first pro match at the age of 14. He was in his first main event, wrestling for the world championship, 10 years later. Lewis earned the nickname Strangler for his feared headlock. This choke hold puts pressure on his opponent's head and neck, cutting off the blood supply to the brain and causing the opponent to pass out.

By the 1920s, Lewis was to wrestling what Babe Ruth was to baseball: a star bigger than the sport itself. Lewis wrestled in main events most of his career, including a losing effort in 1934 against Jim Londos in Chicago in front of 35,000 fans.

GORGEOUS GEORGE (1915–1963)

Richard Wagner from Houston, Texas, was just another wrestler until he decided to become Gorgeous George. His TV debut in 1947 was one of the top moments in TV history, according to *Entertainment Weekly* magazine. His long, blond-dyed hair, fancy robes, and entrance music were just the start. On the microphone, George insulted fans, calling them peasants, and yelled at referees who dared to touch him. For most of the 1950s, George sold out main events and won several championships. He retired in 1962 but not before a young boxer named Cassius Clay (later known as Muhammad Ali) heard George on the radio promoting a match. George made fun of his foe and called himself "the greatest." Ali was inspired by George's sense of showmanship and adopted the boasting style for which he became famous.

Gorgeous George, wearing a silk robe, talks to reporters, fans, and hecklers before entering the ring in 1948.

LOU THESZ (1916–2002)

Legendary wrestler Strangler Lewis discovered Thesz in a Saint Louis, Missouri, gym in 1935. Young Thesz thrived under the training of the former champ. In 1937, at the age of 21, Thesz won his first world championship. But in 1949, he won the most important one: the NWA title. Over the next eight years, Thesz lost only one match! Wrestling was gaining popularity on TV with characters such as Gorgeous George, but Thesz stood out as a serious wrestler who also entertained fans. After losing the title in 1957, Thesz toured Japan and then retired. But retirement didn't last long. Thesz returned to wrestling to beat NWA champ Buddy Rogers in 1962. He would hold the title until losing it in 1966 to Gene Kiniski. At the age of 74, Thesz returned in 1990 for one last match, which he lost to Masahiro Chono. While there may have been flashier wrestlers, few were more respected.

"NATURE BOY" BUDDY ROGERS (1921–1992)

Herman Rohde—better known by his ring name, "Nature Boy" Buddy Rogers—was as tanned and muscled as he was brash and arrogant. He told fans how great he was,

and in return, they jeered him and cheered his foes. Rogers won several championships in the 1950s using his famous figure-four leg lock. In 1961 he beat Pat O'Connor for the NWA Championship in front of 38,000 fans. After winning, Rogers told the crowd in his usual boastful manner, "To a nicer guy, it could not happen." He lost the NWA title in 1962 but became the first WWE World Champion in 1963. He lost that title to Bruno Sammartino

"Nature Boy" Buddy Rodgers puts a choke hold on Killer Kowalski in 1962.

in only 48 seconds! After losing the title, Rogers retired until the late 1970s, when he returned to wrestle a young grappler also called "the Nature Boy," Ric Flair. Much of what Flair became, he learned from Buddy Rogers, a true wrestling original.

BRUNO SAMMARTINO (1935–)

While it took Sammartino only 48 seconds to win the WWE title in 1963, it took him eight years to lose it! He and his family had left Italy during World War II (1939–1945) and settled in Pittsburgh, Pennsylvania. The young Sammartino lifted weights to build up his body. His feats of strength were legendary—most notably his body slam of the 650-pound (295 kg) Haystacks Calhoun. During his career, no man sold out New York City's Madison Square Garden and other arenas in the East Coast more often than Bruno. When Sammartino lost the title to Ivan Koloff in 1971, the crowd at Madison Square Garden sat in stunned silence. Bruno would regain the title in 1973 from then champion Stan Stasiak and defend it until 1977. In 1976 Bruno wrestled a main event against Stan Hansen in front of 30,000 people at Shea Stadium with a broken neck! A champion for more than 10 years, Sammartino is called the Living Legend.

ANDRE THE GIANT (1946–1993)

André Roussimoff was born in France with a rare medical condition called acromegaly. This caused him to grow at a very fast rate. By the time Roussimoff was 14, he was nearly 7 feet (2.1 m) tall. He had huge hands and feet. Roussimoff wrestled main events in Japan and Canada at an early age. He started in WWE in 1973 as Andre the Giant. As a baby face, Andre wrestled and defeated

Andre the Giant climbs into the ring during a 1983 match in Madison Square Garden in New York.

all the top heels. His size made him almost unbeatable in battle royal events, in which wrestlers can be eliminated only by being thrown out of the ring. It's hard to throw a giant over the top rope! No wrestler in the 1970s was more famous than Andre. He appeared on TV talk shows, acted on TV shows, and starred in the movie *The Princess Bride*. In 1987, with his career winding down, Andre wanted a chance to become WWE champion. But he lost in his most famous main event at 1987's WrestleMania against Hulk Hogan. Their rematch in 1988 was the first pro wrestling match on network TV since the 1950s. Andre was more than just a wrestler. With his size and skill, it's no wonder some people nicknamed him the Eighth Wonder of the World.

RIC FLAIR (1949–)

Few wrestlers have wrestled in more main event matches than Richard Fliehr, better known as Ric Flair. He debuted in 1972 and was still active in 2012! Flair won the NWA (later WCW) title 16 times, defeating the likes of Harley Race and Sting. Flair's matches against Ricky Steamboat in 1989 are among the greatest matches ever. Flair won the WWE title at 1992's Royal Rumble when he outlasted 29 other wrestlers. For all his wrestling skills, Flair is known as much for his interviews. With his trademark cry of "whoooh," Flair caught fans' attention and held it. He always said, "To be the man, you got to beat the man," and for more than 40 years in the eyes of many fans, Ric Flair *was* the man.

Flair shows off one his famous robes as makes his way into the ring.

RODDY PIPER (1952–)

Roderick Toombs, known to wrestling fans as Roddy Piper, first gained fame through his role as the heel announcer for Georgia Championship Wrestling. In 1984 Piper joined WWE to do an interview show called *Piper's Pit*. In the show's most memorable moment, he cracked a coconut over the head of wrestler Jimmy Snuka! With his partner Paul Orndorff, Piper lost to Hogan and Mr. T. in the main event at the first WrestleMania. He retired after beating Adrian Adonis at WrestleMania in 1987. Piper came back to WWE and later WCW. His main event against Hogan at WCW's Starrcade in 1996 was one of the biggest PPV events in WCW history. He still often appears on WWE TV to do *Piper's Pit* but hasn't recently hit anyone else with fruit!

RANDY SAVAGE (1952–2011)

With wild costumes, his manager Miss Elizabeth by his side, and his "Ooh yeah" catchphrase, "Macho Man" Randy Savage (real name: Randy Poffo) was an instant hit in WWE. Savage—with a little help from Hulk Hogan—defeated "the Million Dollar Man" Ted DiBiase to win the WWE title in the main event at 1988's WrestleMania. But the friends clashed a year later, after Hogan took Miss Elizabeth as his manager. Hogan defeated Savage in 1989's WrestleMania, and their feud lasted for years. After a brief retirement in 1991, Savage returned to wrestle in WCW. He finished his career in Total Nonstop Action Wrestling before retiring for good in 2005. Savage's unique style made him a pop culture icon. He appeared in the 2002 movie *Spider-Man* and did a series of famous commercials for Slim Jim snacks. His death in a car accident in 2011 saddened the wrestling world.

Randy "Macho Man" Savage *(center)* and his manager, Miss Elizabeth, stand in the ring before a 1987 match in Madison Square Garden.

HULK HOGAN (1953–)

Terry Bollea trained in Florida and started wrestling in 1979 under the name Terry Boulder. With his huge arms, people compared him to Lou Ferrigno, star of the TV show *The Incredible Hulk*. Bollea changed his name to Hulk Hogan and first wrestled as a heel. But fans wanted to cheer this larger-than-life star with tons of charisma. So he began wrestling as a baby face. He built a huge fan base, and soon Hulkamania gripped wrestling fans everywhere. Hogan became a worldwide icon, appearing on magazine covers, in movies, and on TV. He took part in the main event for each of the first nine WrestleMania events! Hogan won the WWE title at the WrestleMania in 1989, 1991, and 1993. After leaving WWE, Hogan became a heel in WCW. He formed the NWO, which led to a huge increase in wrestling's popularity. He returned to WWE in 2002 to wrestle the Rock at WrestleMania in a classic match. Hogan also acted on TV and in movies and had a reality TV show on the VH1 network. Hogan remains the best-known professional wrestler.

STEVE AUSTIN (1964–)

Steve Austin (born Steven Williams) was an instant sensation when he debuted in the Texas-based World Class Championship Wrestling in 1989. Within two years, he won his first WCW title, and his future seemed bright. But his career stalled because WCW president Eric Bischoff didn't think Austin had any charisma. Austin was fired from WCW in 1995 and then joined WWE in 1996. He first wrestled under the name the Ringmaster but didn't really make a splash until he shaved his head and changed his nickname to Stone Cold. After Austin won the 1996 King of the Ring, he cut an exciting, trash-talking interview, and a star was born. Austin's famous feud with Vince McMahon created classic TV moments and huge PPV numbers. Austin retired in 2003, but he still appears occasionally on WWE TV. When his music starts with the sound of breaking glass, fans go wild. They know that, as WWE announcer Jim Ross always said, "business is about to pick up!"

THE UNDERTAKER (1965–)

It starts with the music—a loud chime followed by the spooky sound of an organ. Wearing all black, the Undertaker (Mark Calloway) walks slowly toward the ring in total darkness. Once inside, he raises his hands, the lights go on and the fans go wild because "the Dead Man" is about to do battle. Although the Undertaker debuted at 1990's Survivor Series, he is best known for WrestleMania. As of 2012, he has wrestled in 20 WrestleMania matches and has yet to lose one! His tombstone piledriver finisher has helped him defeat some of wrestling's biggest names, including Triple H and Shawn Michaels. Many fans will never forget the Undertaker's matches in the cell against Mankind or in a ring surrounded by fire against his wrestling brother Kane.

THE BOSS: MR. MCMAHON

Perhaps no man has been more influential in modern pro wrestling than Vincent K. McMahon. McMahon, born in 1945, came from a wrestling family. His grandfather Jess first promoted wrestling in 1915. When he died in 1954, his son Vincent J. took over and made millions promoting wrestling on the East Coast. But one coast wasn't big enough for his son Vincent K., who bought the business in 1982. McMahon made an instant impact on the industry. He convinced Hulk Hogan and other stars to walk out on other promotions to work for him. Loaded with talent and access to cable TV, McMahon ran wrestling shows all over the country and eventually all over the world. He created WrestleMania, the first national wrestling event, and was a pioneer in the cable TV industry. After years of playing the on-screen role of announcer, McMahon became the evil "Mr. McMahon" character in late 1997. His feud with Steve Austin drew record ratings and led WWE to greater riches than ever before. McMahon still gets in the ring every now and then to battle the likes of Hart and Hogan, though he always loses. Inside the ring seems to be the only place he loses, however. He's made billions off his business and all but obliterated the competition.

MICK FOLEY / MANKIND (1965–)

Mick Foley was a huge wrestling fan as a teenager. He and his friends would videotape themselves putting on matches. Foley lacked the athletic look of other wrestlers, so he worked harder and took more risks. He was a master of creating interesting characters and wrestled as Cactus Jack, the goofball Dude Love, and most famously as Mankind. Foley was a hit inside the ring and out, and fans loved the two sides of his personality. In the ring, he was often all business. But he was also the man who introduced fans to Mr. Socko, a hand puppet that he used to drive the evil Mr. McMahon crazy. Always a great communicator, Foley also wrote several best-selling books.

SHAWN MICHAELS (1965–)

In 2010 WWE put out a DVD ranking the greatest wrestlers of all time. Shawn Michaels—born Michael Hickenbottom—was number one. The man known as the Show Stopper and Mr. WrestleMania thrilled fans for more than 20 years. Michaels started out as a tag team wrestler, joining with Marty Jannetty to form the Rockers. But the partnership ended when Michaels threw Jannetty through a glass window! Michaels won many titles in his career, including the WWE title in 1996 when he defeated Bret Hart in a match that lasted more than an hour. Hart and Michaels continued to feud until Michaels beat Hart for the WWE title at 1997's Survivor Series. At this time, he also formed the D-Generation X (DX) faction that ushered in the Attitude Era. After losing the WWE title to Steve Austin in 1998, Michaels retired with a back injury. He returned five years later and soon regained the title. He wrestled until the Undertaker defeated him at 2010's WrestleMania in a retirement match. Many fans shed tears when the Undertaker pinned Michaels and ended his great career.

TRIPLE H (1969–)

Trained by the legendary heel Killer Kowalski, Paul Levesque entered WWE in 1995 as Hunter Hearst Helmsley, which he soon shortened to Triple H. He struggled at first, losing to the Ultimate Warrior at 1996's WrestleMania in less than two minutes. Triple H found his first big success in the DX faction with his female bodyguard Chyna, Shawn Michaels, and the New Age Outlaws. After DX broke up, he formed the Evolution faction with veteran Ric Flair and rookies Randy Orton and Batista. In 2005 he lost to Batista in one of the most watched WrestleMania main events of all time. Triple H's most successful partnership is with Vince McMahon's daughter, Stephanie. They married in 2003 and are expected to take over WWE when Vince steps down.

THE ROCK (1972–)

Dwayne Johnson was a star football player at the University of Miami, but it was always a good bet he'd become a wrestler. Both his father and grandfather had been pro wrestlers, and Johnson's size and build made him a natural fit to follow in their footsteps. Johnson's combination of looks, skill, and ability behind the microphone earned him nicknames such as the Great One and the People's Champion. Fans loved to shout out his many catchphrases, such as "Layeth the smacketh down," "Know your role and shut your mouth," and "You SMELLLLL what the Rock is cooking?" The Rock won many WWE titles and headlined several WrestleMania events before leaving WWE to pursue an acting career. His attack on John Cena at WrestleMania 2011 set up his once-in-a-lifetime match against Cena at 2012's WrestleMania.

REY MYSTERIO (1974–)

Óscar Gutiérrez comes from a wrestling family. His uncle, the first Rey Mysterio, was a huge star in Mexican wrestling. Gutiérrez followed in his uncle's footsteps, wrestling behind a mask under the name Rey Mysterio Jr. When he moved

Rey Mysterio takes a flying leap at Chris Jericho. Mysterio's high-flying moves are inspired by a Mexican style of wrestling.

LUCHA LEGEND: EL SANTO

Mexican wrestling is called lucha libre (Spanish for "free fighting"). In the long history of lucha libre, one name stands above all others: El Santo. Rodolfo Guzmán started wrestling in 1934, the same year the first masked wrestler appeared in Mexico. A few years later, Guzmán donned a silver mask and called himself El Santo. He became more than a wrestler. He became a movie star and cultural hero. From 1958 to 1982, Santo starred in 54 films. His biggest feuds would end with a match where the loser was forced to unmask. But El Santo never lost his mask! Guzmán's funeral in 1984 was one of the largest in Mexican history. He was buried wearing the silver mask of El Santo!

to WWE in 2002, he dropped the "junior," but not the high-flying moves his uncle had taught him. Weighing just 175 pounds (79 kg) and standing 5 feet 6 inches (1.7 m) tall, Mysterio breaks the mold for main event wrestlers. His opponents often double him in size—or more! But when the bell rings, Mysterio flies around like an acrobat, dazzling fans with moves that no other wrestler can pull off. Rey won his first WWE title at WrestleMania in 2006, using his devastating and exciting finisher, the 619. While his face is hidden behind a mask, there's no hiding Mysterio's talent.

JOHN CENA (1977–)

As a child, John Cena dreamed of becoming a pro wrestler. In summer 2002, he joined WWE and made that dream come true. He began his wrestling career as the Prototype. He wasn't an instant success. He was about to lose his job when a WWE official heard him rapping. Cena then took the nickname the Dr. of Thuganomics and entertained fans with funny raps. He quickly rose through the WWE ranks, winning many titles and famously feuding with the likes of Randy Orton and Triple H. Like the Rock, Cena has branched out into an acting career, but the ring remains his true love, and he has no plans to retire anytime soon. He's one of WWE's most popular wrestlers, especially among kids. When he hits the ring, fans know that "the champ is here!"

RANDY ORTON (1980–)

Orton is another third-generation superstar. He made his name as part of Evolution with Triple H, Dave Batista, and Ric Flair. He earned a reputation as the legend killer by beating up Harley Race, Mick Foley, and other all-time greats. At 24, Orton became the youngest WWE champ. While his first title reign was short, Orton rode the power of his RKO finishing move to become one of the best and most popular wrestlers in WWE. Nicknamed the Viper, Orton represents the best of a wrestling champion: unique moves, a great look, and great skill behind the microphone. Like Frank Gotch and all the other greats before him, Orton has the *it* factor—a charisma that sets him apart and earns him a spot in the main event.

Randy Orton *(left)* puts opponent, Kane, into a headlock during a match in Sydney, Australia, in 2006.

RISING STARS

Within WWE, new stars are always emerging. The Miz transformed himself from a reality show star to a wrestling superstar in a few short years. CM Punk gained experience working in small promotions such as Ring of Honor. Daniel Bryan won titles in Japan and also wrestled in the Ring of Honor before coming to WWE. Mexico continues to be home for second-generation stars such as Alberto Del Rio, whose father Dos Caras wrestled in main events in Mexico for years. Sin Cara is also the son of a famous Mexican wrestler. These are just a handful of the young talent in WWE who will ensure that main events will be filled with action and drama for years to come.

4 WRESTLING'S MOST DEVASTATING FINISHING MOVES

Characters, personalities, and dramatic stories are a big part of wrestling. But what many fans really want to see is *action*. To be successful, a wrestler needs to be able to pull off the moves that make the fans gasp and cheer. No superstar wrestler is complete without his own set of specialized signature moves, from simple punches and kicks to complicated and dangerous finishers.

Most wrestlers are best known for their finishers. As the name suggests, these are the moves a wrestler breaks out when it's time to finish off an opponent. Some finishers, such as the figure-four leg lock, are submission holds. Their purpose is to make an opponent submit, or quit the match. Moves like the 619 are designed to knock out an opponent long enough to get a pin. From Strangler Lewis's headlock in the 1920s to Buddy Rogers's figure-four in the 1950s and John Cena's STF finisher, devastating finishing moves win matches.

The best wrestling moves are also some of the most dangerous. WWE cautions its fans not to try these moves on their own. Wrestlers spend years training to gain the strength and skill needed to pull them off safely. When untrained fans try them, the consequences can be disastrous. As WWE says, don't try these at home.

THE STF

Wrestling fans go wild when John Cena busts out his famous stepover toehold facelock. But what many don't know is that this famous finisher dates back to Lou Thesz, who used the move late in his career.

To do an STF, Cena gets his foe facedown on the mat. He wraps his foe's ankle between his legs. Then Cena wraps his hands around his opponent's chin. He pulls back hard, putting pressure on the legs, shoulder, and neck. From this position, all he has to do is pull until the opponent submits.

FIGURE-FOUR LEG LOCK

Buddy Rogers invented the figure-four leg lock in the 1940s, but Ric Flair perfected it. Flair gets his opponent to the mat with a series of leg-weakening moves. Once his opponent is down, Flair grabs his opponent's legs. He steps over one leg as he bends the other. With his leg placed between his opponent's legs, Flair drops to the mat. His foe's legs get locked up in the shape of the number four, which gives the move its name. The pressure on the legs becomes so intense that Flair's opponent has no choice but to give up.

619

In the early 1980s, the 160-pound (73 kg) Satoru Sayama took Japanese wrestling by storm with his acrobatic moves. Wrestling under the name Tiger Mask, Sayama invented the tiger feint kick. Rey Mysterio later borrowed the move. It was renamed the 619 for the area code of his hometown, San Diego.

To pull off a 619, Mysterio wears an opponent down and then knocks him into the ropes, facing outward toward the crowd. Mysterio then bounces off the ropes on the other side of the ring to pick up speed. He races across the ring, leaps into the air, and grabs the middle rope. He spins in the air, and his legs slam into the face of his opponent, who falls back into the ring. It's a devastating move that Mysterio usually turns into a three count and another victory.

RKO

One mark of a good finishing move is that it can be used anytime on any opponent. A move like the figure-four leg lock is hard to use on someone as big as the 500-pound (226 kg) Big Show. But Randy Orton can use his RKO on an opponent of any size. The RKO resembles the diamond cutter made famous by WCW wrestler Diamond Dallas Page. It was actually developed by Johnny Ace, an American wrestler working in Japan. Orton charges his opponent and then quickly turns his back. He snatches his foe's head and leaps, kicking his legs in front of him. At the same time, he lifts his opponent off the mat. As his opponent lands, Orton smashes his foe's head into the mat. That earns the move its name: *R* for Randy and *KO* for knockout.

Randy Orton performs his signature move, the RKO, during a 2011 matchup against Christian.

PILEDRIVER

The piledriver has been a big part of pro wrestling since the 1940s—even though many states once banned it for being too dangerous. NWA world champion "Wild" Bill Longson used this spine-crushing move to win hundreds of matches. One of the most famous piledrivers came at WCW's Wrestle War in 1989. Terry Funk attacked Ric Flair outside the ring. They both stood on a wooden table. Funk kicked Flair in the stomach, and Flair bent over at the waist. Funk stuffed Flair's head between his legs and then grabbed onto Flair's trunks. He pulled Flair toward him so that Flair was upside down! Funk jumped while holding Flair's head between his legs and crashed into the table! The Undertaker uses a modern version of this move, called the tombstone piledriver. He holds his foe upside down so the top of his foe's head is at his knee level. The Undertaker then falls to his knees. This drives the other wrestler's head into the mat. If it's done properly, a piledriver usually means the end for an opponent.

PUMP IT UP

Not all cool moves are finishers. Sometimes the purpose of a move is to pump up the crowd. Few wrestlers do this better than the Rock with the people's elbow. For this move, the Rock gets his foe on the mat and stands over him. He takes off his elbow pad and throws it into the cheering crowd. The Rock bounces off the ropes, jumps over his fallen foe, and then hits the other ropes. He pauses for a second to soak in the crowd noise and then drops his elbow hard onto his opponent's chest. John Cena's five-knuckle shuffle is a similar move in both execution and the excitement it builds for the fans.

SWEET CHIN MUSIC

The standing savate kick has been a part of wrestling for decades. Wrestling fans often called it the superkick. But no one could pull it off like Shawn Michaels, whose version is called sweet chin music—although there's nothing sweet about being kicked in the face! Michaels waits until his foe is tired and then "tunes up the band" by stamping his foot on the mat to get the crowd to respond. He lifts his leg toward his chest as he lowers himself to the mat. When his foe walks toward him, Michaels kicks his foot out with all his weight behind it. The kick lands on his opponent's chin, sending him sprawling—often out cold—to the mat.

MOONSAULT

Nothing pumps up fans like seeing a wrestler climb to the top rope. They know that a big move is coming up. Top-rope moves date back to the 1950s, when Edouard Carpentier and other high-flying wrestlers thrilled fans. Over the years, these moves have continued to evolve, especially among Mexican and Japanese wrestlers. One of the best is the modern top-rope move is the moonsault. The moonsault landed on U.S. shores in the late 1980s when the Great Muta wrestled for WCW. Kurt Angle pulled off one of the most impressive moonsaults against Mr. Anderson in a 2010 cage match. After knocking Anderson down in the center of the ring, Angle climbed to the top of the cage! With his back to the ring 15 feet (5 m) below, Angle jumped high in the air. He kicked his feet out and did a somersault before landing on top of Anderson. It's an exciting and powerful move, but it takes a toll on both wrestlers!

THE SLEEPER

The sleeper is one of the simplest and most effective holds in wrestling. The idea is to cut off the blood supply to the brain by applying pressure against the arteries in the neck. If blood does not get to the brain, a person passes out. Strangler Lewis's headlock was an early sleeper hold. Roddy Piper won his 1987 WrestleMania match against Adrian Adonis with a sleeper.

Roddy Piper subdues Chris Jericho with his sleeper hold in their 2009 WrestleMania match.

Piper got behind Adonis and wrapped his arms around Adonis's head. One arm pushed down on the top of the head, while the other wrapped around the chin. The pressure against the head and neck caused Adonis to pass out.

GTS

Like the moonsault, CM Punk's GTS (go to sleep) is a Japanese import. Developed by Japanese star KENTA, the GTS takes both strength and skill to execute. Punk lifts his foe onto his shoulders using a fireman's carry, a simple amateur wrestling move. Punk pushes his opponent up and drops him. But rather than just let the opponent smash back down on the mat, Punk brings his knee up, smashing it into the falling man's face. It's a complicated move that few can execute. Punk uses many knee strikes based on martial arts moves. And when he does, it's time for someone to go to sleep.

STONE COLD STUNNER

Perhaps no wrestler won more matches with his finishing move than Stone Cold Steve Austin. The stunner starts with Austin kicking his foe in the stomach, forcing him to bend over. Austin turns his back to his foe and presses his opponent's head against his own shoulder. Austin leaps in the air and lands in a sitting position. The other wrestler's chin crashes hard into Austin's shoulder. But not only wrestlers have fallen to the stunner. In addition to every member of the McMahon family, even billionaire businessman Donald Trump got "stunned" at 2007's WrestleMania!

Steve Austin performs his legendary Stone Cold stunner on Booker T during a 2011 WrestleMania event.

5 WRESTLING'S MOST MEMORABLE MOMENTS

Some might argue that everything about pro wrestling is weird. With its unique characters, bizarre story lines, wild costumes, and over-the-top moves, there's always something interesting going on. Some of this wackiness is—and should be—forgotten. But other wild stunts stick in the minds of wrestling fans forever. They help shape the future of wrestling and remind fans why they love watching pro wrestling. Keep reading to learn about a few such moments.

KILLER KOWALSKI TAKES OFF YUKON ERIC'S EAR

Killer Kowalski was an early star of network TV wrestling. He traveled around North America, challenging local heroes to matches. In Montreal the hero was ring veteran Yukon Eric. Eric suffered from a condition called cauliflower ears. His ears had become so swollen from rubbing up against the mat that they resembled a cauliflower. During a 1954 match, Kowalski had Eric tied up in the ropes.

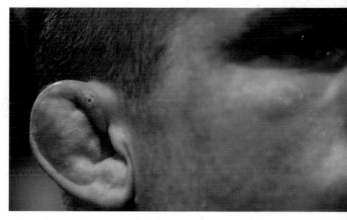

This photo shows cauliflower ear, a condition from which Yukon Eric suffered. Cauliflower ear is common among wrestlers.

Kowalski climbed to the top turnbuckle and then hurled himself down toward Eric. Kowalski's shin hit the side of Eric's head. The move didn't knock Eric out, but it did tear the ear right off his head! Kowalski lost the match, but at least he kept all his body parts!

GORGEOUS GEORGE SHAVES HIS HEAD

For most of the 1950s, Gorgeous George sold out arenas all over the United States and Canada. Near the end of his career, he wrestled mainly in Los Angeles, California. With his trademark long, curled, blond hair, he proclaimed himself the Toast of the Coast. But he was not the champion. A masked wrestler known as the Destroyer held that honor. Fans wanted to know who was behind the mask. So George challenged the Destroyer to a match with unusual stakes. If George won, the Destroyer would have to take off his mask. If the Destroyer won, George would have to shave off his beloved hair. More than 8,000 fans crowded into Los Angeles's Grand Olympic Auditorium in November 1962 to watch the big match. The action went back and forth. Fans, who normally hated George, were cheering for him to win. They wanted to see the man behind the Destroyer's mask. But they didn't get their wish. After a tough match, the Destroyer locked George into a figure-four leg lock. George had no choice but to give up. Fans watched as George shaved off his long hair in the middle of the ring. The gorgeous one became the bald one!

Big Boys, Little Bikes

Pro wrestling is famous for its huge athletes. But even a giant like Big Show looks tiny compared to the McGuire twins, who wrestled all over the world in the 1960s. Benny weighed 814 pounds (370 kg), while his twin brother, Billy, was 784 pounds (356 kg)! In the late 1960s, Honda hired the twins to promote its new line of minibikes. The highlight of their matches was the strange sight of two huge men riding tiny motorcycles toward the ring!

GORILLA MONSOON TAKES ON MUHAMMAD ALI

In 1976 boxing champ Muhammad Ali was sitting in the front row at a wrestling card in Philadelphia, Pennsylvania. The 400-pound (181 kg) Gorilla Monsoon knocked his foe outside of the ring in front of Ali. Ali yelled at Monsoon and jumped into the ring. He threw jabs at Monsoon, but they landed short. When Ali tried another punch, Monsoon grabbed Ali's arm, lifted Ali onto his shoulders, and put him in an airplane spin! Monsoon spun and finally slammed Ali hard onto the mat. Dazed and dizzy, Ali ran away. The Gorilla made a monkey out of the world's greatest boxer!

JERRY LAWLER SLAPS ANDY KAUFMAN

Andy Kaufman was a popular comedian and actor in the early 1980s. He wrestled women as part of his comedy act. In 1982 Kaufman took his act to Memphis, Tennessee. There, he wrestled women and insulted wrestling fans. Memphis champ Jerry Lawler challenged him to a match. Lawler lost when he used a piledriver, which was an illegal move in Memphis. The comedian was carried from the ring on a stretcher! Months later, the two were guests on the TV show *Late Night with David Letterman*. Kaufman wore a neck brace. He claimed Lawler had injured him. The two argued until Lawler slapped Kaufman's face. Kaufman threw coffee on Lawler, who then chased Kaufman off the TV set. Letterman's fans went crazy. They had never before seen anything like it on his show. Was it real or was it staged? They didn't know what to believe.

ANDRE BEATS HOGAN WITH TWIN REFEREES

The famous 1987 WrestleMania match between Hulk Hogan and Andre the Giant was only the beginning of a long feud. The two were ready to tangle again in February 1988 for the return of pro wrestling to

Actor Andy Kaufman lies passed out in the wrestling ring after going head-to-head with Jerry Lawler in 1982.

prime-time network television. Hogan was the baby face. Andre—managed by " the Million Dollar Man" Ted DiBiase—was the heel.

The back-and-forth match lived up to the billing. The Giant beat up Hogan but couldn't pin him. Hogan "hulked up" and fought back as fans cheered. But Andre was ready. He slammed Hogan to the mat and went for a pin. Referee Earl Hebner began the count, "One." Then Hogan raised his shoulder, which should have stopped the count. But Hebner kept counting! "Two. Three." The bell rang and Hebner raised Andre's hand. At that moment, another referee charged out toward the ring. It was Dave Hebner, Earl's twin brother. Dave was supposed to be the referee, but DiBiase had paid Earl to take his place and give Andre the victory. An angry Hogan

Donald Trump *(center)* poses with Hulk Hogan and Andre the Giant before 1988's WrestleMania.

picked up Earl and tossed him out of the ring! It was one of the strangest finishes to a wrestling match, and it happened before the largest TV audience in WWE history.

HULK HOGAN TURNS HEEL

Hulk Hogan was a baby face for most of his WWE career. In 1993 Hogan left WWE and joined WCW. He kept up his winning ways, defeating Ric Flair for the WCW title in Hogan's first match! He continued to beat up on the heels of WCW, and Hulkamania ran wild. In 1996 heels Scott Hall and Kevin Nash came to WCW. Billed as the Outsiders, they challenged three popular WCW wrestlers (Sting, Randy Savage, and Lex Luger) to a match. Hall and Nash said the third member of their team would be revealed during the match. As the match neared its finish, the Outsiders were in control. Hulk Hogan charged to the ring. Fans cheered, believing that Hogan would take care of the heels. But instead, Hogan attacked Savage, allowing Hall and Nash to win! As fans threw garbage into the ring, Hogan insulted them and announced the start of the New World Order (NWO). It was the most shocking turn of baby face to heel in wrestling history.

THE UNDERTAKER THROWS MANKIND THROUGH THE CELL

Mick Foley debuted in WWE as Mankind by attacking the Undertaker in the ring. It was the start to a long feud between the two. In 1998 WWE wanted to settle the feud once and for all. Their solution was to bring back the rarely used cell match.

Mankind came out first. Rather than walking into the cell, he climbed to the top of it! When the Undertaker arrived, he followed Mankind to the top. The two fought on top of the cell, high above the mat. The Undertaker grabbed Mankind and tossed him off the cell! Mankind sailed 20 feet (6 m) down and crashed through a table. Despite being injured, Mankind climbed back to the top of the cell. The Undertaker wrapped his hand around Mankind's throat for a choke slam. When Mankind hit the top of the cell's roof, he crashed through it and fell to the mat! While Mankind would lose the match, the images of him flying off the cell—and then through it—won him a place in wrestling history.

LESNAR AND BIG SHOW BREAK THE RING

A June 2003 *Smackdown* match featured a battle of giants, with Big Show taking on former college wrestling star Brock Lesnar. After almost 10 minutes of action, Big Show knocked Lesnar to the mat and then climbed the turnbuckle in the corner. But before Big Show could leap from the top rope, Lesnar got to his feet and climbed the same ropes. With both wrestlers on the top of the turnbuckle, Lesnar wrapped Show's head under his left arm and grabbed the back of Show's tights with his right. Lesnar lifted Show over his head for a suplex slam off the top rope. The force of their combined 800 pounds (363 kg) was more than the ring could handle. The turnbuckles collapsed, the ropes fell in, and the mat crashed to the floor. A dazed referee looked on as Lesnar and Big Show lay on the sunken mat. It was one of the most amazing sights ever in WWE.

EDGE CASHES IN MONEY IN THE BANK

At WrestleMania in 2005, WWE unveiled a new kind of match: the Money in the Bank match. It was a ladder match with six wrestlers. The goal was to climb the ladder and grab a briefcase hanging above the ring. The case contained a contract that allowed the winner of the match to challenge for the WWE Championship at any time.

To win a Money in the Bank match, a wrestler must climb a ladder in the center of the ring and grab a briefcase.

The six men fought for 15 minutes. Bodies flew everywhere! In the end, Edge grabbed the case. He carried it with him and waited until the right time. Finally, at New Year's Revolution in January 2006, Edge saw his chance. WWE champ John Cena had just defended his title against five other wrestlers. Fans thought the event was over, but McMahon came out and announced that Edge was cashing in his Money in the Bank title shot! Edge came into the ring and speared the tired Cena to win his first WWE Championship. In later years, watching a Money in the Bank winner take out an exhausted champ would become commonplace. But that first time, fans—not to mention Cena—were shocked to see Edge become the champ in a matter of seconds.

THE ROCK RETURNS TO WRESTLEMANIA

The Rock left WWE in 2004. But in January 2011, he returned as the host of WrestleMania. For weeks before WrestleMania, the Rock appeared on *Monday Night Raw* to make fun of Cena's clothes, his movies, and even his fans! Cena tried to shut him up by body slamming the Rock hard in the ring. But that only made the feud grow.

During the final moments of 2011's WrestleMania match between John Cena *(left)* and the Miz *(right)* steals the spotlight by delivering his rock bottom move to Cena. The Miz went on to win the match.

Cena wrestled WWE champ the Miz in the WrestleMania main event. The two took their fight outside the ring. When both wrestlers failed to return to the ring, the ref counted them out. But the Rock came to the ring and announced that the match would continue. There would be no disqualifications. Cena and the Miz returned to the ring where the Rock was waiting. The Rock wrapped his arm around Cena's neck and did his rock bottom slam! Cena crashed hard into the mat, and the Miz quickly covered for the pin! The Rock may have gone Hollywood, but he showed Cena he could still lay the smackdown on anyone at any time.

The next night on *Raw*, Cena challenged the Rock to a match in 2012's WrestleMania. For a year, the two trash talked on television and through social media. But the time for talk was done when the two icons met in the Rock's hometown of Miami, Florida. The men battled for 20 minutes in front of 70,000 fans in a match loaded with near falls and submission attempts. Cena seemed to be in charge when he hit the Rock with the Rock's own move, the people's elbow. But the Rock recovered just in time. He got to his feet and used his rock bottom slam to win yet another main event.

6 LOOKING FORWARD:
THE FUTURE OF PRO WRESTLING

In 2011 Vince McMahon changed the name of his company from World Wrestling Entertainment to WWE. McMahon no longer wanted the word *wrestling* associated with his company, claiming that there was no future for wrestling, only for "sports entertainment." But even if McMahon changed the name, he has not changed what happens in the ring. It is still professional wrestling. And in the United States, WWE *is* professional wrestling. The future of wrestling depends upon the future of WWE.

EXPLAINING THE DECLINE

Many fans believe that wrestling's popularity peaked with the Monday night wars of the late 1990s and early 2000s. The fierce competition between WWE and WCW led to a high-quality product, and many fans were fiercely loyal to one promotion or the other. But WCW closed in 2001, and no real competitor to WWE has surfaced since. Impact Wrestling (formerly called Total Nonstop Action Wrestling, or TNA) has been in business since 2002. The company has tried to compete with WWE, hiring wrestling legends such as Ric Flair, Hulk Hogan, and Mick Foley. But Impact's ratings are a fraction of WWE's and its PPV business doesn't even compare.

Smaller promotions such as Ring of Honor and Dragon's Gate are known only to hardcore wrestling fans. They run PPV events, but only on the Internet. Some small local promotions don't broadcast TV shows at all. Instead, they just do live shows before audiences in school gyms, bingo halls, and other small venues. Often these small promotions hire one former WWE or WCW wrestler and fill out the card with young, inexperienced wrestlers. CM Punk and Daniel Bryan started with such groups.

Some fans point to the rise of mixed martial arts (MMA) to explain wrestling's waning popularity. MMA provides fans with a lot of the same excitement as pro wrestling, along with lots of colorful characters. But it has the added advantage of being real competition. It's sport rather than sports entertainment. The Ultimate Fighting Championship (UFC) is the top MMA promotion. UFC has a booming PPV business, consistently outselling WWE. There is some crossover in both fans and competition, however. Brock Lesnar, for example, has held titles in both WWE and UFC.

Others blame wrestling's decline on a lack of new stars. Wrestling's popularity is driven by characters, and explosions in its popularity tend to follow the arrival of a new star, such as Hulk Hogan or Stone Cold Steve Austin. The rise of John Cena has helped WWE,

Frank Mir *(left)* and Brock Lesnar *(right)* duke it out in an Ultimate Fighting Championship event in Las Vegas in 2009.

NOT SUITABLE FOR KIDS?

Wrestling is often filled with violence, sexual imagery, and harsh language. For decades, people have questioned whether it's suitable for children. After a riot in Madison Square Garden in 1957, children were banned from attending wrestling there for more than a decade. Many people argue that ban should still be in force. Some are concerned that children aren't ready to handle the adult themes in wrestling. Others worry that kids will try to imitate wrestlers, copying dangerous moves as well as the asocial behavior that is part of many wrestling characters.

Others are critical of wrestling because of its history with drugs. In the 1970s, "Superstar" Billy Graham and other wrestlers abused steroids to help them build huge muscles. In the early 1990s, Vince McMahon was put on trial for distributing steroids. While he was not convicted, many wrestlers, including Hulk Hogan, admitted to steroid use. The physical demands of wrestling have caused some wrestlers to abuse painkilling drugs, an addiction that contributed to the deaths of wrestlers Eddie Guerrero, Brian Pillman, and Curt Hennig.

but it needs more and bigger stars. WWE is constantly looking for the next big thing. It works with Florida Championship Wrestling (FCW) to train young wrestlers. The reality TV show *Tough Enough* brings new talent to WWE. Wrestlers from Ring of Honor, including CM Punk, have gone to WWE. But none of these wrestlers have captured the public imagination the way Hogan, the Rock, and Austin once did. And until WWE finds a character to rival their popularity, it's likely the company will continue to struggle.

RAYS OF HOPE

While the picture in the United States may look grim, WWE is gaining in popularity in other parts of the world. Its popularity in Mexico and Japan is surging. When WWE tours Europe, Australia, or India, the crowds are huge. Likewise, more and more viewers outside the United States are tuning into PPV events. In May 2011, for the first time, WWE took more orders for a PPV event from outside the United States than it did from within. WWE has even started to run shows in China, the most populous country in the world. WWE's shift to a global focus may be a driving force in its future success.

One question that lingers over WWE is its future leadership. Many believe that Vince McMahon is nearing retirement. He may eventually turn over control of WWE to his daughter, Stephanie, and her husband, Paul Levesque (better known at Triple H). While WWE is a family-run company, it is no longer totally owned by the McMahon family. In early 2000, McMahon sold stock in his company to the public and, with it, a measure of control.

For decades, people have predicted the fall of pro wrestling. But every time the sport looked doomed, it came back stronger than ever. New stars and new ways of reaching fans have always been the key. Wrestling first flourished when network TV began and then again at the start of cable TV. Closed-circuit broadcasts, pay-per-view, and DVDs all helped carry wrestling to new audiences. What is the next big thing? How will wrestling take advantage of the Internet and social media to reach new fans?

What happens in wrestling is very simple. Those who love it require no explanation of what makes it so compelling. For those who hate it, no explanation will matter. Wrestling endures because it is time-tested storytelling. Two men wrestle in a ring as thousands of people watch. One represents good, the other evil. One might be big, the other small. The more entertaining the wrestlers, the more people want to see them battle. This has been true since Frank Gotch and George Hackenschmidt locked up in Chicago in 1908. For true fans, watching pro wrestling is really all about the magic moment when the ring announcer says, "Ladies and gentlemen, it is now time for your main event."

GLOSSARY

angle: an incident that furthers the story between two wrestlers, such as a backstage attack

Attitude Era: a period during the late 1990s when WWE featured mature story lines aimed at adults

baby face: a wrestler who fans view as a hero

cage match: a match that takes place in a ring surrounded by a metal cage

card: the list of matches that take place during a wrestling show. The card starts with the opening match and builds toward the main event.

cell match: similar to a cage match, but a cell has a top as well as metal sides

charisma: charm or personal appeal that inspires devotion in others

disqualification: also called DQ, the ending of a match due to a rule being broken. A championship does not change hands if the champ loses by DQ.

faction: a group of wrestlers who work together, such as the New World Order

feud: an intense rivalry between two wrestlers

finisher: a move that a wrestler uses to finish off an opponent and end a match

foe: an opponent or an enemy

heel: a wrestler who most fans view as a villain

hold: a move in which one wrestler controls another wrestler, normally by grabbing onto one body part, such as a headlock

Monday night wars: an intense competition from 1995 until 2001 in which WCW's *Monday Nitro* and WWE's *Monday Night Raw* battled for TV ratings

pay-per-view: also called PPV, a technology that allows fans to pay to watch a premium wrestling event on TV

produce: to oversee the creation of a TV show, movie, or other entertainment event

promotion: a company that produces and promotes wrestling

ring post: one of the four posts at each corner of a standard wrestling ring

signature move: a move or hold for which a wrestler is well known

slam: a move in which one wrestler throws another wrestler hard onto the mat

submission hold: a hold designed to force an opponent to give up, usually due to intense pain

tag team: a pair of wrestlers who fight as a team

tap out: a way for a wrestler to indicate that he is submitting. The wrestler taps the mat when he is ready to give up.

title: the wrestler who is the champion and wears the title belt

TitanTron: a large video screen used by WWE to show videos or backstage interviews

turn: when a wrestler changes from being heel to baby face, or baby face to heel.

turnbuckle: a device used to set the tension of the ropes in a wrestling ring. Each corner includes turnbuckles, which are covered in soft padding.

FURTHER READING

Books

Alexander, Kyle. *Pro Wrestling's Most Punishing Finishing Moves*. Philadelphia: Chelsea House, 2001.

Black, Jake. *The Ultimate Guide to WWE*. New York: Grosset & Dunlap, 2011.

Page, Jason. *Martial Arts, Boxing, and Other Combat Sports*. New York: Crabtree Pub., 2008.

Rickard, Mike. *Wrestling's Greatest Moments*. Toronto: ECW Press, 2008.

Sullivan, Kevin. *The WWE Championship: A Look Back at the Rich History of the WWE Championship*. New York: Gallery Books, 2010.

Wells, Garrison. *Amateur Wrestling: Combat on the Mat*. Minneapolis: Lerner Publications Company, 2012.

Websites

How Pro Wrestling Works http://entertainment.howstuffworks.com/pro-wrestling.htm
This site covers everything from history to the rules of pro wrestling. Filled with photos, illustrations, and links, the site is a great starting point to learn more.

Impact Wrestling http://www.impactwrestling.com/
If you want to learn more about Impact Wrestling, this is the place. Find photos and biographies of popular wrestlers, news, information about upcoming matches, videos of past matches, and much more.

Pro Wrestling Hall of Fame http://www.pwhf.org/index.asp
This is the official site for the Professional Wrestling Hall of Fame (PWHF) in Albany, New York. Check out the Hall of Famers section to learn more about the greatest pro wrestlers of all time.

Pro Wrestling Illustrated http://www.pwi-online.com/index.html
Pro Wrestling Illustrated magazine is packed with all kinds of information on professional wrestling. Tons of photos, news stories, and features make it easy reading for hardcore wrestling fans.

ROH Wrestling http://www.rohwrestling.com/
Learn more about Ring of Honor wrestling at its official home page. Read about ROH's most popular wrestlers and upcoming events. Check out photos, videos, wrestling blogs, and much more.

WWE http://www.wwe.com
The official site of the WWE is loaded with information and features. Learn about popular wrestlers, upcoming matches, and the history of WWE. Check out photos, videos, podcasts, and much more.

WWE Title History http://www.wwe.com/inside/titlehistory
Want to know whether your favorite wrestler has ever held a WWE title? This is the place! This page lists every wrestler who has ever held a WWE title, from current belts such as the WWE Championship and World Heavyweight Championship to belts that don't even exist anymore.

INDEX

ABOUT THE AUTHOR

Patrick Jones has been at times in his career a librarian, consultant, trainer, and novelist, but he has always been a fan of professional wrestling. His first published work was at the age of eight in the wrestling newsletter *In This Corner*. One of the highlights of his career was interviewing professional wrestler and *New York Times* best-selling author Mick Foley at a library convention. He can be found online at www.connectingya.com—except on Monday nights, when he's watching the WWE on TV.

Photo Acknowledgments

The images in this book are used with the permission of: AP Photo/Rick Scuteri, pp. 4, 29; © Science & Society Picture Library/Getty Images, p. 6; © NY Daily News Archive via Getty Images, pp. 8, 10; © Charles Hoff/NY Daily News Archive via Getty Images, pp. 9, 32; © Jon Fischer/Independent Picture Service, pp. 1 (title type), 10 (background), 22, 37, 40, 45, 50 (background), 58; © Globe Photos/ZUMA Press, p. 11; © Mike Lano, wrealano@aol.com, pp. 13, 18, 20, 21, 23, 24, 25, 26, 28 (both); Dana Edelson/NBC/NBCU Photo Bank via Getty Images, p. 14; © Ethan Miller/Getty Images, p. 15; Library of Congress, p. 17 (LC-USZ62-57542); AP Photo/FS, p. 31; © Michael Abramson/Liaison/Getty Images, p. 33; © Bruce Bennett/Getty Images, pp. 34, 35; © Steve Grayson/WireImage/Getty Images, p. 39; © Don Arnold/WireImage/Getty Images, p. 41; © Panoramic/ZUMA Press, p. 44; © Bill Olive/Getty Images, pp. 46, 54; Paul Abell/AP Images for WWE Corp., pp. 47, 55; © Al Bello/Zuffa LLC via Getty Images, p. 49; © Keystone Features/Hulton Archive/Getty Images, p. 50; © Thomas Busler/The Commercial Appeal/ZUMA Press, p. 51; © Russell Turiak/Getty Images, p. 52; © Josh Hedges/Zuffa LLC via Getty Images, p. 57.

Front cover: © Bob Levey/WireImage/Getty Images; © Jon Fischer/Independent Picture Service (title type). Front cover flap: © Daniel Berehulak/Getty Images (top); © Globe Photos/ZUMA Press (bottom).

Main body text set in Adobe Garamond Pro Regular 14/19.
Typeface provided by Adobe Systems.